AF255570

Plea$e Steal Me for 100 Plus Dollar-zz

a plea in twenty-ONE panels

Kirsten Mosher

LILY POETRY REVIEW BOOKS

For Fletcher

(please me) (eat me) (hot-stuff)
(sweet-stuff) (you choose) (kick-ass)
(crazy4you) (peace-out) (free love)
(butt-talk) (be mine) (rock me) (...)
(you choose) (my baby) (your baby)
(home-sick) (feel me) (true-love)
(hug me) (all mine) (only me) (call me)
(sweet talk) (xox) (let's kiss) (soul-mate)
(stuck-on you)

<3

(please me) Please Come to Dinner at
(eat me) It's the most marvelous place.
The address is (hot-stuff)
I mean POBOX:
ITISASMALLPLANETAFTERALL
Everyone is invited
Right NOW.

<3

**If the Puffiness of Destruction
is Hurting You** (sweet-stuff)
Get Out of the Lovely Zone.
(you choose)

<3

MY chemicals don't match
MINUS Off-brand organs
PLUS discount inhales
EQUALS
(kick-ass)
WINNER TAKES ALL.

<3

YOUR RAINBOW WRAPPING PAPER
SMEARED WITH MY GLITTER GLUE
WINS THE TODAY PRIZE!!!
(crazy4you)

The Sun Doesn't Usually Look Like That
And I was running which is cool,'cause
THAT is not how I stand.
INSTEAD
PRETTY SOON &
the floor is fine. (peace-out)

That was for yesterday
Now it's OOOPS DAY.
My Long Red Beams
will reach you way more than
T H E   O T H E R   C O L O R S
(free love)
@SaveitfortheSunset
ALL THE TIME.

<3

If that reminding me from cell towers
(butt-talk)
Doesn't work,
It's Oh OK.
MY freebie.

I will not ask for anything, but
Float me down
On the Gassy Love Boat
Of your Utterances…(be mine).
My soul-ish-ness is lodged in the Loch.
Please (rock me).

<3

(...) I APOLOGIZE FOR

____

fill in your pixel

Sincerely,
TODAY

I got so love squishy,
I can now fit through
Any slit under closed doors,
or getting out apparatus.
That is very For REAL
Without any symbolic accessories.
All Night and All right,
(you choose).

<3

I Never Stopped Staring Anymore for
VALUE-PIECES.
(my baby)times(your baby)
Plea$e Steal Me for 100 Plus Dollar-zz.

WHEN THEY SAY
POLLUTION MAKE ME HAPPY,
you say
POLLUTION MAKES ME (home-sick).

<3

It still bothers me to think about Blowing Up.
(feel me)

<3

Arnold the Terminator is
Eating a Jelly Doughnut and
(true-love) TO THE RESCUE
But she's lost in the sky, &
She's Baby-Blue.
That's the moment I looked
And Looked Up
And noticed
Nothing
4-Ever.

<3

I didn't think
There are
That many
First days
Of school.
(hug me)

<3

It is ALWAYS hide and seek
in their Vertical Throat Offering.
(call me) for extra tomorrows
And now I'm, forgot our names
But that's cool.
I'll never-mind from the bus stop.

<3

Remember (sweet talk)
That's when Your/
My sticky fingers
Got in the way, and
Smearing stuff, so
Don't clean it off in your mouth.
That's not the job.
PLUS
Your Winking Eye is so cool from NOW ON.

WATCH OUT!
It is not your antenna
feeling it up for THE CAUSE
the rules are:
show that you care,
sign your name here
for ever more. (xox)

<3

And the people are thinking
When WE go outside
It is ALWAYS past the expiration date.
so (let's kiss).

<3

RIGHTON is still inside
The Lovely Zone
Or Get Out
While You Can. (soul-mate)

<3

Thank you for Letting Me
wheat-paste my STORY
On to Your SCREEN. (stuck-on you)

www.ingramcontent.com/pod-product-compliance
Lightning Source LLC
Chambersburg PA
CBHW042054030726
47599CB00019B/2489